RICH WIFE

WISCONSIN POETRY SERIES

Sean Bishop and Jesse Lee Kercheval, series editors

Ronald Wallace, founding series editor

Rich
Wife

EMILY BLUDWORTH DE BARRIOS

The University of Wisconsin Press

Publication of this book has been made possible, in part, through support from the Brittingham Trust.

The University of Wisconsin Press
728 State Street, Suite 443
Madison, Wisconsin 53706
uwpress.wisc.edu

Printed in the United States of America

Library of Congress Cataloging-in-Publication Data

Names: Bludworth de Barrios, Emily, 1983– author.
Title: Rich wife / Emily Bludworth de Barrios.
Description: Madison, Wisconsin : The University of Wisconsin Press, 2025. |
Series: Wisconsin Poetry Series
Identifiers: LCCN 2024039577 | ISBN 9780299351649 (paperback)
Subjects: LCSH: Women—Poetry. | LCGFT: Poetry.
Classification: LCC PS3602.L833 R53 2025 | DDC 811/.6—dc23/eng/20240909
LC record available at https://lccn.loc.gov/2024039577

This book is dedicated to the women who cook the meals,
set the table, serve the food, and fill the glasses before, finally,
sitting down to serve themselves

What I wanted was a baby in my arms, a home, a husband,
a kitchen to cook in, a yard to raise roses.

MYRA LEWIS WILLIAMS

✦

But the widow who uses her life to please herself is really dead
while she is alive.

1 TIMOTHY 5:6

✦

One day the fierce wolf that walks by my side will spring on you
and rip your abominable guts out.

JEAN RHYS

Contents

RICH WIFE

Grandmother Worship

Hat box, pillbox, pillbox hats

Patsy Cline is like a ribbon unwinding all across the kitchen

Put your head inside a hair dryer shaped like a giant egg

Mauve carpet, pink carpet, carpet to carpet an elegant dream

One's future!

Like wallpaper

Like being one of those people who has—wallpaper!

Can you imagine?

As a girl cleaning pig intestines, who could have imagined?

As a girl using bathwater first used by grandpa, grandma, elder brothers

"You never wanted to be last"

Errant hair in tepid water

Now a house with mauve carpet

And snapdragons and peach trees and peach cobbler

Gold earrings where you can exchange different colored hoops to match
your shirt, belt, shoes

If you wish

And she does

Red loops, yellow loops

A narrow waist

"A sweater girl" once upon a time

Left home at 14 to become a live-in maid

"My daddy wasn't a nice man"

Imagine you have vomit in your mouth and you don't want anyone
to know you have vomit in your mouth

You have that feeling all the time

She had that feeling all her life

My grandmother brushed her hair and applied lipstick

As my mother brushed her own hair and applied lipstick

And I brush my hair and apply lipstick

I brush my daughter's hair and she marvels at my painted fingernails,
wonders when she can wear lipstick

The girls

Nipped at by men's eyes

Licked by the edge of a gaze

A stranger touched you with his look and it made you feel like an expensive
thing in a store that someone would eventually knock over and break

As you were eventually knocked apart by tumbling out of the hayloft and
sunburns and the lawnmower accident and the years stacked up together
and your husband's new lover who was so nice, such a supportive second
wife, your hair coming in gray, your teeth rotting out, a lump which could
be cancer, which was cancer, being cut out, the baby who didn't make it
left behind among those years, who never came out chubby and alive

My two grandmothers

One wore gloves to church and cat eye sunglasses and Jacqueline Kennedy
dresses

The other wore loops of beads and pearls over lime green suits

Lime green lies at the center of a bright dream

Where the future fizzes in acid tones

It's cool man, take it easy

Swinging in tomato red, avocado, and hot orange

A grandmother drags the past into the future

Dragging catfish through the batter

Punching discs for biscuits from damp dough

A flour-dusted surface

Frying bacon in the center of Patsy Cline caterwauling about her broken heart

You're in the forest of weeping willows of a wailing broken heart

Your youth broken on the pavement of the 40s

The shards of the 50s

Your beautiful dresses disintegrated like your skin, loops of skin, dreams or years sloughed off

Having gotten a dog for the children

Having sent the children off to play

Rubbing cream into the skin of your neck

Leaking out through the seams

A pitcher of Bloody Mary, a well-loved garden, a freshly cleaned catfish, a house that announces one has finally arrived

A better world promised by advertisements on TV

The round baritone of a man's voice

A fat-burning device, a toaster, an egg-shaped hairdryer to dry your hair

After the Great Depression, the war

A woman needed a man to "take her away from all this"

Hormones fizz and sing

Ice cream in a dish on a table in the kitchen

A handsome man in a serviceman's uniform

A handsome man perched on the edge of a barstool

Peanut shells on the floor

Brushing your hair and applying lipstick in the light of a single bulb

Crickets and frogs singing out there in the dark

While the world is still young

Collecting Sticks

The girls wore the names of their fathers like little necklaces

The boys wore the names of their fathers like jewels I mean like tattoos

The names of the mothers fell off

Like how a bird's nest erodes inside months

It's okay   Months are always making new girls

Girls make themselves into new mothers the way a bird collects sticks

The girls wear their fathers' names and then inscribe their husbands' names: a tattoo of a necklace around the throat

The names of the mothers fell off

Pryor   York   Bond   Moore

There aren't any others I know

Mama York making biscuits in her little wood-burning stove

A mother didn't have a name to bestow

The mother an antique lullaby   A nest is only made of sticks and spit
and dirt

A sweet voice breaks down into soil

Shouting into the closed-off years

Dies.   and here's another little self

Who dies.   and pushes a piece of herself into the future

Rich Wife

The rich wife

Waking amid

Walking among

Like hatred   A basket of coals

A garland of derision

Sip a special coffee cup full of her

The world's riches pushed into certain piles

In this neighborhood a lump of money

(None in that, completely flat)

The constable sends weekly emails to the residents informing them
of how he's protecting them

How he's protecting them

A leisurely roll   through the neighborhood

Meanwhile the laundry is sorted into different piles

Blacks pile   Reds and pinks pile   Yellows pile   Jeans pile   Whites pile   Creams pile

The rich wife is like the worst sort of creature

Like an ancient queen   Let them eat   free & reduced lunch

She doesn't say at a dinner table

But she feels it   "Magnanimous"

There's a type of creamy white dove with a deep red chest like a pierced wound

A garland of decisions

The rich wife is not a rich wife

Shuffles   Slouches   Lisps

Stands behind the other mothers at swim class

Their chestnut hair shimmering   Fingernails shining

The rich wife does not have an allowance, exactly

Does not hide her expenses, exactly

More like a secret set of sounds

Needs bleat pitifully beneath the day

Beneath the day   The purchase is a balm in time

Like perfect weather

Or any other miracle

Time gathers

In little piles melting behind her

The purchase is a palm tree waving in a fantasy

Tattered fronds flutter in a cheering breeze

Once they traveled to a resort on an island and practiced being happy

In a suite of hotel rooms

Cleaned by invisible women

The rich wife nods to the invisible women with the

The rich wife nods to the invisible women (invisibly)

(The rich wife does not like the music at the resort piped from speakers disguised to look like rocks)

(She does not like "the limbo" being led down on the beach)

(She does not like the gluttony of the cafeteria, does not like "cafeterias")

(Cannot peel back the surfaces of her snobbery)

The rich wife has not cleaned a toilet since

Of course

The rich wife writes a book everyone will hate

Everyone will hate

Hatred seethes in oozing glossy pools

Sweep your hatred into little piles

And what will you do with your hatred?

The rich wife peels back her mind and dissolves it in steaming water

She calls this watching TV

Or reading a book

That is how she sheds being the

Surprise   A rich wife does not have much time to

A checklist pierced with crossed-out lines

A checklist pierces her peace of mind

She closes her list of worries

You with your list of worries simmering

In text can be found a type of catharsis, people say

If hoarding wealth is immoral

The rich wife is blessed with a distracted mind

She closes her list of worries

If hoarding wealth is immortal

The rich wife is less like an ancient statue of carved stone being whipped with sand for thousands of years

The rich wife is both "rich" and a "wife" in the same way that one is alive:

Temporarily

Like standing on a very little raft in the center of the ocean

The rich wife is the most despicable creature in the world

Whirled emotions rise when considering the rich wife

Chiefly among them: derision, disgust, antipathy

The rich wife feels a sense of embarrassed scorn when anyone begins to "show off"

When anyone begins to brag about money

She feels queasy when anyone asks about someone's "last name"

Sending forth   some little signals

Or not sending signals forth   Merely   Really

Ascertaining the social order

The rich wife is not really   a rich wife

If richness is something you carry in your mind

Her mind is more like a shopping mall

There are "rich people's secrets" and the rich wife doesn't know them

She remembers lip gloss and hallways lined with lockers

And "sucking in"

(And a boy who said in science class, of a girl who wasn't there,

"Opening her legs was like opening a book")

She remembers puka shell necklaces

Gelled hair with bleached tips

(Carefully combed from back to front)

The rich wife was one boring shell of a person among 1,200 boring shells

Can't you tell?

Can't you tell from reading her thoughts now?

The rich wife was never a boy in science class announcing

"Opening her legs was like opening a book"

The rich wife was assessed, like a book

Discarded, stolen, perused

The rich wife was a stupid girl

She layered eyeshadow on her eyelids

(Like light glittering on the ocean at night)

She lined her lips in lip liner

If she had had an imagination, she would have dreamed of ocean liners slicing the dark sea

She imagined—nothing

She imagined being looked at and felt cold ice pour down the back of her neck

The rich wife felt cold ice pour down the back of her neck

At swim class   among the nannies and mothers   stamping like thoroughbreds

If richness is something you carry in your mind

If richness is immoral

If richness is immortal

The statues of the ancient rich thrust their shoulders back like

White creamy marble

Marble that looks like hard milk

Or

Sandstone flecked with wind

Nefertiti was a rich wife

And Livia was a rich wife

(Her head in statues frothy with hard round curls)

(Her slender neck improbably supporting a tall cylindrical crown)

Mary Delany, rich wife and dependent widow, her chubby old face framed with a white bonnet

As a widow cutting thousands of pieces of minuscule colored papers to compose photorealistic "mosaiks" of flowers

In the 18th century

Red poppies burn from inside a black square

The tangled mind of a passionflower waves its tendrils in Mary Delany's depiction of it

"the story starts when the artist was 72"

The rich wife bides her time

Cultivates some skills

Within some constraints, a life

The rich wife picks up shoes

The rich wife lines up the shoes on the shelf above the labels of the children's names

(Yellow shoes, blue shoes, strawberry-red shoes)

She puts a cheesecake in the refrigerator to chill

She lays out 5 dinner plates 5 forks 5 glasses large and small

The rich wife enters a children's birthday party into her calendar

Enters a dentist appt into her calendar

Enters "bring two pumpkins to school" into her calendar

Hangs the homework bag on the doorknob

Puts a container of sliced cucumbers into the snack drawer

Tilts back the blinds to shed sunlight onto the children's aloe vera

Some true stories

One

A rich wife is made into a widow

And is made destitute by the ineptitude of her sons

Two

A rich wife is made into a widow

And makes an empire of her dead husband's company

(Faces death, conquers debts)

Three

A rich wife   Now a widow

Dedicates her life to preserving her face   Donating to charities in her own honor

Four

A rich wife   Now a widow

Writes her third or fourth book

About how the 19th century grips the rich wife

(Her vapid deadened life)

In her book Madame Pontellier touches her own bare arms in a borrowed room in a little house

In a bright fresh hot afternoon on the Gulf Coast in 1899

Kate Chopin writes

> *Edna, left alone in the little side room, loosened her clothes, removing the greater part of them. She bathed her face, her neck and arms in the basin that stood between the windows. She took off her shoes and stockings and stretched herself in the very center of the high, white bed. How luxurious it felt to rest thus in a strange, quaint bed, with its sweet country odor of laurel lingering about the sheets and mattress! She stretched her strong limbs that ached a little. She ran her*

fingers through her loosened hair for a while. She looked at
her round arms as she held them straight up and rubbed
them one after the other, observing closely, as if it were
something she saw for the first time, the firm, firm quality
and texture of her flesh. She clasped her hands easily above
her head, and it was thus she fell asleep.

The rich wife stretches in the very center of the bed

In a stolen moment, in a borrowed bed

Edna carrying her hair like a rich burden

Edna carrying her hair like a burdensome beauty

Health   wealth   youth

The arms of the rich wife belong to her children

Who love her and clamber upon her

The burdensome beauty of her children

Her children are glaring miracles shining in her face

She is lucky to have such rich burdens

She was once herself her mother's sweet burden

Etc

Back and back throughout time

The little girl sleeps in the crib

Her long hair clotting her face

The rich wife reels   Without moving

In the little hours she could find

On one end of sleep a child was crying

On the other end of sleep a child was crying

The rich wife stretches a nest between these two points of time

The children of the rich wife peel back the rim of her brain

To feed on what she grew there herself

The rich wife is an archetype without a shred of humanity

Like a cow who is also a pet

The animal whose fur will be brushed but whose flesh we will not eat

The barn a little cube of comfort

The animal's shoulders will never lean into the kind of work that matters

At which point the metaphor breaks

What kind of work matters

Whose pain

Edna's arms reach upward through time

Her children's nanny does not reach her arms upward through time

She is struggling to get Etienne and Raoul into bed when they would prefer to continue sword fighting with sticks

In other words her time is occupied, edge to edge

At 17 the rich wife is a nurse to her husband who is 60 and sick from drinking

At 43 the rich wife

At 72 the rich wife

Mary Delany's layers of paper flowers burst from the dark

✦

The rich wife bursts from the dark   into the midst of her life

Into the middle of her life

She nods to the invisible women (invisibly)

It's a little easy to be magnanimous inside long mornings

A long morning settles in like a blue sky over

Los Angeles
or
Houston
or
Santa Cruz
or
London
or
Cairo
or
Beirut

Blue the color of a painful thought

"I cut myself upon the thought of you" Amy Lowell wrote

Not a rich wife but a rich daughter   who did not become a rich wife

Here I am in a library 100 years later

Squinting at Ezra Pound who called her a "hippo-poetess"

Amy in a mansion   Amy among flowers

(Mary Delany writing of her own flowers in 1748)

("the enamelled look they have is rich and pretty")

"Sevenels" was Amy Lowell's ancestral mansion

"Dream Drops" was a book she made as a little girl

"I cut myself upon the thought of you"

She wrote of a passionflower in her poem "Granadilla"

(To cut oneself by merely imagining another)

And who did she imagine?

The woman surrounded by soft plush hunks of money

Amy handsome in a man's coat   Amy sailing down the River Nile

"I cut myself upon the thought of you

And yet I come back to it again and again"

Soft plush hunks of money

The rich wife nods invisibly to the rare rich unmarried women smoking
cigars in the mansion

(Smoking cigars with their friends)

The rich wife nods to the dignified women

Who live inside long long mornings

Kate Chopin gave birth to six children in eight years

A widow at 32   Inheriting her husband's failures

The new widow nods to the women

Who live inside long dignified mornings

The rich wife nods to the women

And squints at the ancient husbands

✦

In his museum house in Hartford

One can walk the long room Twain used as his writing room

(And office and billiards room and bar)

(A windy nest with wind entering at any of the three windows or balconies)

(Wind to blow cigar smoke away)

(His butler's living quarters only steps away)

(Invisible hands to sweep dishes away)

(What a mess of glass and ashes)

One floor down is the schoolroom of his daughters

Two floors down is the reception room

The domain of his rich wife

Entirely pastel creams and pinks, like a collection of shells

Unlike the Tiffany foyer which is a dizzy dark galaxy

And the conservatory which is a green jewel of light

And the library which is lush with rich rugs & stories

To be in her reception room is to be inside an egg with smooth walls

Across the lawn is the house of Harriet Beecher Stowe (rich daughter)

Thinking of Jane Austen (rich daughter)

Of Zelda Fitzgerald (rich wife)

And Virginia Woolf (rich daughter)

(Woolf among swans and old gray bricks)

And Louisa May Alcott

And Edith Wharton in her mansion writing of Lily Bart:

"She made no reply, but her face turned to him with the soft motion of a flower."

"She could not figure herself as anywhere but in a drawing-room, diffusing elegance as a flower sheds perfume."

"She was like some rare flower grown for exhibition, a flower from which every bud had been nipped except the crowning blossom of her beauty."

The rich wife & heiress in her library resting on the bodies of other women

Writing her book

Rich means pearls, cut flowers, drawing rooms, new coaches

Rich means a domicile, a conveyance, freedom from destitution

Or freedom from fear of immediate destitution

Or freedom from near-term hypothetical destitution standing on your
shoulder with its wet persistent breath

Rich means

At the end of her story Lily Bart (emerging from Edith Wharton's mind)

Dies (destitute, of overdose or suicide)

"she had been brought up to be ornamental"

Had been dismissed by the milliner

(Without some money) (to carry on)

The rich wife nods to the women who lived destitute

"much deteriorated"

(To work a small job for a drab salary)

(To return to a little room with thin walls)

(And insects which come out at night)

(The rich wife knows this too)

✦

The story is always some variation of this:

The woman was a writer's muse

The woman was an artist's model

She was also his domestic servant

She managed his career capably

(She was an artist in her own right)

She was his lover, or his mistress, or his wife, or

She was a financial dependent the artist had sex with

She has no children

She has 8 children

She has a husband who died

She is a charwoman

She is a barmaid

She makes hats

The artist fell in love with her when she was 10

The artist fell in love with her when she was 12

The artist fell in love with her when she was 14, with ribbons still hanging down her back

The artist was disgusted by her "person"

Upon first meeting her, the art critic wrote "she gave me her hand, as a good dog gives its paw"

She died in a nursing home at the age of 27

She died in an insane asylum

She "received electric shock treatments, during which she broke several bones after falling off the operating table"

He found her "much deteriorated"

Her likeness slicks calendars and postcards and living room prints

In paint an exaggerated form of ideal beauty

Circe Ophelia Guinevere Lilith

She never recovered

✦

I was born into a time when women were almost liberated

I was born into a time

We put chemicals on our hair to make it curl

Chemicals on our hair to make it straight

With metal clamps or tongs we made it crimp, or roll, or flat

Imagine a doll that has a person inside it

Imagine a human who wakes curled in the head of a doll

I open her eyelids like this

Like this I move her arm

Hippie doll
Glamour doll
Slutty doll
Retro doll
Barbie doll
Jem doll
Skater doll
Grunge doll
Shops at The Gap Is a Wholesome Ideal doll
Going to a Good College doll
Top of Her Class doll
Caught Smoking Cigarettes in the Parking Lot doll
Uses Cuss Words doll
Ruined doll

Used doll

Seductively Corrupted doll

In the case JESPERSEN V. HARRAH'S OPERATING COMPANY

Darlene Jespersen testified

> *She did not wear makeup on or off the job and said that*
> *"wearing it would conflict with her self-image." She found*
> *the makeup requirement offensive and saw it as further*
> *evidence that Harrah's "'sells' and exploits its women*
> *employees." She "felt very degraded and very demeaned,"*
> *claiming that the makeup requirement "prohibited [her]*
> *from doing [her] job" because "it affected [her] self-dignity"*
> *and "took away [her] credibility as an individual and as a*
> *person."*

The heading of the *Harvard Law Review* article reads
TITLE VII—GENDER DISCRIMINATION—NINTH CIRCUIT HOLDS THAT
WOMEN CAN BE FIRED FOR REFUSING TO WEAR MAKEUP.

The case was decided April 14, 2006

The dawn of the 21st century

I was born into a time

Imagine a doll that has a person inside it

I dress the doll thusly

If my doll is very pretty

If my doll pleases

What does a doll create?

A doll waits patiently for accolades & accomplishments

A doll a delusion an invisible accomplishment

How to be more gentle   more genteel

A doll proffers her hand when introduced to an accomplished man

He squeezes the tips of her fingers, oddly

Or he refuses to relinquish her hand until she introduces herself properly

To bear the skin of a doll is to wear an inferior type of costume

Its power is diaphanous, permeable, wavering, temporary

It is a power that turns and collapses

A doll is a stupid metaphor

A woman cannot climb from the skin of a doll

"I felt very degraded and demeaned"

"It affected my self-dignity"

✦

In these paintings the women have thick strong bodies, like a column

Their skin is like an inanimate material: marble, bronze, jet

Her hair, a river of fire

Her hair, a cloud of smoke

Her face barely emerges from the surface of a dewy green pond

Enchantress, seductress, witch, wife

Green velvet, cream silk, crimson flowers

Paintings of women with no women inside them

✦

Circe turns Odysseus's men into pigs

Circe   with power inside her   dispenses with the rage born of impotence

Takes up the mantle of the rage of revenge

Circe pouring a green bowl of poison

Circe circled by lions who used to be men

The rich wife pours a dish of liquid green rage into the waters of

The rich wife daubs up seepages of rage

A green rage seethes

"A queen"   announces the Pre-Raphaelite painter upon spotting a new model

"I have found a queen"

The queen wields her beauty like a chrysanthemum just beginning to wilt

The woman who was a queen proffers now a wilted flower

The rich wife closes down her mind

Daubs away the remains of her own green thoughts

The rich wife folds the children's clothing   changes the baby's diaper

Nods to the invisible women who are scouring the countertop's cool black stone

A melodrama of rage washes away with water

"We accept the reality of the world with which we're presented"

The rich wife wants to protect the women who are now ghosts

The rich wife wants to protect the women who

Humiliation seethes

Pressed flat by the economy humiliation seethes

The men's accomplished paintings shimmer from postcards and gallery walls

The women's less accomplished paintings are displayed in special shows

(The galleries echo with the women's missing works)

(The masterpieces they never made)

(With techniques they were never trained in)

(Perfected with time they never had)

✦

The classical rich wife descends from a plane with tanned and well-shaped legs

Her closet is modeled on her favorite stores

An emphasis on space, preservation, soft light, display

The eternal purity of the object emanates a soft creamy light

The classical rich wife is well-lit, demure

She married a count, a president, the CEO of a weapons manufacturer

Here she is at the birthday celebration of a European prince

Her ego is always showing   Her ego is never showing

Her husband wishes she

Her ego in the shape of her shoes, her son's exclusive school, the location of her home, the thousands of Christmas lights wrapped around the 100-year-old live oak trees that thunder in a line across her front yard

Her coveted handbag   Her thick mane

Sometimes an ethereal comfort in

Demure at her husband's side, at the company Christmas party catered in their home

Demure at the public event where cameras whir with loudsoft clicks

The classical rich wife adheres a type of admirability

Respectfulness   of her pensive, gentle beauty

Her absence

She has no part in his success   No part in his crime

She slips from beneath the veil of his crimes like a

One never sees her in a coffee klatsch

The classical rich wife doesn't complain, or clean

Doesn't complain in public

The classical rich wife lives inside the shape of a woman

She herself remains missing from view

An ego is a house with long tall columns

The columns reference classical civilizations

In the myths of classical civilizations rich wives are famously dangerous

In some cases, the ego is a gullet whose appetite never ceases

In other cases, what appears to be ego is an ambition to survive

That isn't accurate   I mean an ambition to thrive

The rich wife cannot hear your accusations of exploitation

She lives in a neighborhood with a gate

In her front living room she is closing the curtains now

Or a woman who works for her is closing the curtains now

She herself remains missing from view

✦

Peel back the edge of an accomplished man

And you will find his household has been managed for him

He does not even need to manage the woman who manages it for him

(She manages herself, like any animal)

He opens his closet: pressed white shirts appear, steamed wool suits appear, hung in separate sections, left to right

The kitchen stocks itself, so it seems

Milk eggs meat cheese glass bottles of Gerolsteiner, coffee tins, sugar

Cooked meals at dinner; cooked meals preserved in glass receptacles in the fridge

Fresh sheets on the bed

Children, who attend a school, whose teeth are brushed, who bring specially selected wrapped gifts to birthday parties, with handwritten cards

His children, who say "thank you," who dress themselves, who can carefully sound out the words in a book

The man walks into a room: the furniture has been arranged just so, the television remote put into a little basket

Like magic   Not magic

(Like a creature from a fairy tale)

(The world is readied in anticipation of him)

Now he must work   At his elbow, everything appears

His coffee, his pencil, his book   His important and difficult work

✦

Of the rich wives I know, something bad has happened to each

It isn't my place to say what

✦

It isn't my place to say what

✦

This is very retrograde, isn't it?

Isn't this inaccurate?

✦

At night on a beach nearby a woman was walking all around her
the inhalation and the exhalation of the surf the ocean heaving in a
continuous soothing respiration

This happened 50 years ago

Again, it isn't my story to tell

✦

23 years ago a girl was jogging alone

✦

Or

She was on a date

✦

She was on a date

✦

She was working the overnight shift in a hotel

✦

Of the women I know, something bad has happened to each

It isn't my place to say what

✦

Isn't this inaccurate

The woman who is either wife or not wife strikes out into the world

With her diploma in her hand..........

With her ambitions

Of which she has complete control

She speaks with authority

And confidence

She doesn't contort herself

Doesn't use a heating device to smooth her long hair.........

Doesn't alter the color of her hair, her teeth, her skin, her lips, her lashes

Doesn't make her voice as small as a child's

Doesn't coax her person

Or trim her voice

✦

At night on a beach nearby

A woman was walking

All around her the inhalation and the exhalation of the surf

The ocean heaving in a continuous soothing respiration

In this version of the story

I have altered the shape of society

At night on a beach nearby

A woman was walking

All around her the inhalation and the exhalation of the surf

The ocean heaving in a continuous soothing respiration

In this version of the story

A woman is walking at night on a beach nearby

And nothing happens to her

She's fine

✦

The face of the rich wife ages gracefully

The face of the rich wife ages monstrously

On the shining pages of celebitchy.com we love to see how power breaks
under a botched surgery

They made monsters of themselves, we like to watch their face emerge like
a creature from a lake

✦

We made monsters of ourselves

(And who is "we"?)

We wanted the best of everything

We wanted our whims and our tumultuous emotions stimulated then
smoothed into the soft roar of a surf

✦

(Inside the hatred of the rich wife

Is a hatred for wealth

And inside the hatred of wealth

Inside the rich wife is a little pocket to stuff a hatred of women

We love to watch her scandalous court case fill the headlines

Her unbelievable closet stuffed with shoes

We like to watch her stuff her body into clothes

The gray bloated face

To arrange her hair her face into a shape that makes her still good

We relish the failed attempt)

✦

The classical rich wife has two duties:

    (1) To maintain her household

    (2) To maintain her beauty

To shield her husband from the shame of a deteriorated wife

To shield her skin from ultraviolet light, to file her nails, shave unsightly hair, to keep her appointment with the trainer and the dietician, inhale up, a photofacial, exhale down, weighing her food on a scale

(On the Valle Arriba golf course in 1998 one girl gestured to her mother in an overlarge hat)

("My mother" she rolled her eyes and sighed)

("That hat")

("She just had a facelift")

("She can't get sun on her face")

(One girl's mother knows the source and course of shame)

(How it settles on a family like water in a valley)

✦

Like water in a valley

"We accept the reality of the world with which we're presented"

So a girl collects cosmetics

Collects advice from magazines

Collects a man a house a set of children a means to continue on

Stands behind the other mothers in swim class

Collects her husband's pressed shirts, his steamed suits

Prepares a treat

Serves the foods her children love

Marmalade   morning light   honey dripping from a spoon

✦

Nothing but derision for a selfish stupid woman

✦

The girl chooses to become a rich wife

Or the girl is chosen to become a rich wife

Or the girl is not chosen to become a rich wife

Commonly the girl has no ambition to, no interest whatsoever

Sometimes a girl chooses the shape of her life

Commonly she does not

✦

Pearls in a cup   Tapers in brass

Hair pins and hat pins   Vials of perfume

Zinaida Serebriakova paints herself *At the Dressing Table* in 1909

Jaunty confident healthy and pleased

Gripping her mane in her fist   Running the black comb through

Dressing gown   Pitcher   Basin   Linens

(At the public exhibition in 1910, painter Valentin Serov calls her self-portrait a "very cute and fresh thing")

The portal or the viewpoint of the painting is the mirror of her dressing table

(The painted wooden edges of the mirror visible at the edges of the painting)

Therefore in looking at the painting we are looking in a mirror

(We are briefly Zinaida Serebriakova confident and alive in 1909)

✦

Occasionally the story is a version of this:

Before marriage

Before dying in childbirth when she was 30

Before losing all the sources of her income

Before the birth of her sweet children

Before the stillbirth

Before the laudanum

After she leaves the art critic and the painter

After she enrolls herself in a separate school

After her children grow up

After she secures a separate source of income

After becoming a widow at the age of 72

A woman preserves a piece of her mind for posterity

The Pelvic Bone

Passing through the pelvic bone as if passing through a grand mansion

At what other point does one pass through a doorway of bone

Then the mother feeds reads pleases teaches urges pleads recedes

The mother teaches one example of a life

The mother teaches one example of a life (hers) and another example of a life (that which one ought to aspire to)

An actual life and its shimmery shadow

An aspirational self   smiles graciously, sits perfectly square to the table, says thank you, writes thank you cards

An aspirational self   graciously chides the actual self   An aspirational self chides the actual self through gritted teeth

Like paper silhouette cutouts of two different people, one cannot match them   There is the self one is and the self one wants to be

✦

Passing through the pelvic bone as if

I was within someone, now I am without

The mother grips the child dripping it with attention

I love you I love you I drip attention upon you

You are covered with the drops of my attentions

In one smooth movement the head turns, the eyes come to rest upon you

Attention, as they say, is a form of love

Oh not any attention   The crowd curls its lips and loves to feel disgust

You are not its child

Gripped in the drips of attention

Passing through the pelvic bone

Or being lifted up through a slice

The child taken up   A miracle a miracle

The woman pinned like a specimen   The mother doesn't die

The child doesn't die

A series of pelvic bones

Millions of pelvic bones   set end-to-end

Form a tunnel of time

We are always at the end of history   birthing it anew

Conditions improve   Conditions decline

The mother is like a science project, and then a nurse

The mother is like a vial, then a shawl

A blanket, a mantle, a pair of arms

I have been a happy vial

Nauseated laid upon my side

I didn't fall

The babies came out

A sweet miracle

A baby looks ancient in its wisdom   curled and resolute

Already   at once   a self-contained container

A child is another country

I'm here peering in at the border

✦

Ilium: "the broad, upper portion of either hipbone"

Ilium, a bone like two gestures, a bone composed of "wings"

A bone like two hands held in front of the chest, rotating outward

A gesture like a word meaning "khalas" "basta" "enough"

Like miming "away"

Ilium: "Latin name of ancient Troy"

Like: I am emerging from ancient soil

From ancient soil the body is composed

From ancient culture the mind is composed

Like a pot broken and abandoned / broken and remade / broken and
buried / broken and mended and set in a special display case / broken and
ground to dust

The gestures of my mind composed of dust

With water making the dust into new clay, etc

A new ancient vessel

Your venerable form

A form of grace you possess is the shape of your mind

I am paying attention to the shape of your mind

Your particular way of arranging the dishes on the drying rack

Your memories like vessels you carry inside you

Afternoons and sunlight warm against your back

Years and schooldays rimmed with emotions

Passing through the pelvic bone to claim your inheritance

Sacrum: the five last vertebrae fused to form a single bone

Sacrum, sacred, holy

I'm sensitive to the vibrations of the house

Little feet padding down the hall

The woman swerves her attention back to the task at hand

✦

Passing through the pelvic bone

Here at the outset we are already two

We are already almost two

The child's body does not belong to me   (though I am bigger)

I do not belong to the child   (except I do)

I relinquish my legs my lap my arms my hours my hours of sleep that begin in the evening and end at dawn

I relinquish my bladder my priorities my attention my thoughts appearing like loose strands

I wrap the strands of my thoughts around   "dinosaurs"   and   "flower press"

And "matching the pieces in the painted wooden stacking set"

At bedtime, I wrap the strands of my thoughts around a hug and release them into the night

Passing through the pelvic bone as if weeping vast tears of milk

The mother carries the child as if it were an expensive sack of burden

A heavy sack of silk and silver

A frost of delight limns the rim of her small sleeping body

Passing through the pelvic bone into silver light and moon

Passing through the pelvic bone into mother, lights, room

Passing through the pelvic bone as if the moon is a circle or a crescent
that symbolizes your childhood forever hanging in the sky

The girl is the woman who carries the girl

Well   I did wear a hot pink backpack

I did   when there were still lightning bugs   capture lightning bugs in a jar

What a stupid thing to write about

Their dim bulb winking weeping off and on

In the dim grim grinning list of perpetual delights

The list that's rimmed with glints of sadness

Like flashes of metal in the sun the slap of my hand getting a mosquito

The sweet smell of *Off!* at summer camp

Girl talk and friendship bracelets at summer camp   At that time

I read the classic novels that described life and in them life was riveting
and unrecognizable

I read the teen fiction that was tingling with the suggestion of desires that
were only implied

I read serialized stories packaged in lavender, pink, yellow, pale tangerine, muddy pale blue

Tales of a perfect false life unfolding at the lip of the sea

At the lip of the Pacific Ocean

Boys and malls and mix-ups and sports cars and parties and meanwhile

At the mall I would hand the receipt back with the product and say, "Thank you have a nice night" and the man would say, "It would be a lot nicer if you came home with me"

Or at the mall my friend would say

And I would say

And my friend said

Back then the boys we knew decorated their bedroom walls with posters of women kissing or women wearing low-rise jeans or sometimes only sand

At the beach the sand was mixed with   oil   traces of oil   broken green beer bottles worn into an oval   a palm   a shape of an ear

Sand containing the dead bell of a jellyfish and the dead bell of a jellyfish and a single broken claw

In my culture motherhood was a far-off goal

Not a goal

An impediment   A burden

Discussed like so: "domestic chores are still unevenly divided"

"Don't be stupid" or "college" or "get yourself knocked up" or "premarital sex" or "Girls Gone Wild"

Pulling pantyhose up and over my legs in a long skin-like tube

Pantyhose a long shimmering neck

Pantyhose with a run   caught on the sharp edge of your rough nail

Pantyhose black   Pantyhose white   Pantyhose Mary Janes and sailor collars on Easter Sunday

Sliding among the legs of adults drinking coffee out of Styrofoam cups

Adults milling about like monoliths like shadows and mountains and entities that last

Milling among the women in lipstick and wigs and Aqua Net and belted silk violet garments

Womanhood was permanent: the feeling and distance of the moon

Girlhood was a twin bed

Motherhood silver rippling ephemeral light reflecting upon the sea

The mother carries the child as if it were a sack of silk and silver

A frost of delight limns the rim of her small sleeping body

The ears soft as worn sea glass

Passing through the pelvic bone the girl is dipped in the color of silver

Passing through the pelvic bone the girl rips the mother's skin and muscle

Passing through the pelvic bone

The ears soft as worn sea glass

The mother is dipped in salt ripped dripped in blood given at the hospital one adult-sized diaper

Wearing that diaper filled with blood the mother fits the child into its little diaper

Fits the Velcro across the abdomen its little torso tight as a water bottle filled like a drum stumbling to the bathroom the baby's awake the mother pulls herself from her car into Walgreen's to buy more diapers for the new girl

In the stirrups on the table the mother's numb legs feel like the strong soft legs of somebody else

The mother who was the girl is somebody else / somebody's mother / herself / another self she inherited / battered about by the years

Passing through the pelvic bone

The mother full of sleep

Her legs are a little town and her shoulders are a town that's switched off its lights

A town dark and asleep in the evening the mother covers her eyes with a gray sleep mask

Now the child crawls in at the crook of her arm / light the color of gold in the crook of her arm

(To the girl the girl feels like silver)

(To the mother the child feels like gold)

Light as warm as the color of gold pools in the crook of her arm

The mother plucks out her "self" a portion of her "self" to place on the nightstand

Like the book or the project   something she means to get back to

✦

Passing through the pelvic bone as if weeping vast tears of milk

Passing through the pelvic bone into arms, crib, and quilt

Passing through the pelvic bone the girl begins and ends

The girl begins and ends and then she wends her way

The baby she was the baby she was her sweet yellow girlhood

The girl sends herself

Wends her way among the

Don't say "obstacles"

Among the bittersweet pieces of knowledge she discovers hanging in
the television set, in the fashion pages that shine like sliced peaches, like
pomegranate broken open

The perpetual list of delights thrums among her

To be a girl was not a bad gift

It is not really a bad gift

If you wash it and brush it and comb it and spread lotion upon it and
cloak it from the sun it is not such a bad gift

If you attire it in a faultless way

What is "faultlessness"?   A cloud a beautiful cloud hanging just beyond
over there at the rim

That cloud is shining is bursting with light

Pomegranate is the most beautiful fruit

Gems or jewels full of aching red light

Aching red light   The famous story of pomegranates is

Persephone whose crime was   disobedience?   or hunger?

Eating Gushers in 1994 the red liquid bursting through

The girl is given a miniature plastic woman

The little plastic woman

This is your future

Her fitted cat eye sunglasses

Her black and white knitted bathing suit

The dolls like the fashion magazines like the serialized books the color of
dinner mints

Minuscule white linen halter

White motorcycle jacket from another era

Blue stilettos

Yellow little sandals

And a neon pink swimsuit

For an imagined pool party the girl believes she will one day host sizzling

The blue pool a wavering jewel

✦

Passing through the pelvic bone into a glimmering afternoon

Passing through the pelvic bone into quivering light and gloom

Into various kinds of doom

I put doom into a book and leave the book elsewhere

I put doom into a book

I give the list of perpetual delights a look

The resurrection fern bides as a thousand curled dried fingers then unfurls into shaggy sweet green dangling after a rain

The hundred large ant hills thriving on the median that leads to Interstate 45   are spaced apart at least 6 feet, each with a queen

Delight is the after-school library program where the girl goes or the boy goes and there entering among several of a hundred thousand worlds

Blue carpet   skylight   honey oak

To thrive a little while, and look

The mind of a book, the shape of its gate

Passing through the gate I picked a phrase and made it my excuse to be with you awhile

✦

Horizontal golden bars of golden sun

I am slicing onions then I am reading then I am holding a child on my hip

The List of Cloying Delights

Inside it I am knitting and chopping vegetables and wiping the counter down, and the sink

The ideal mother is made entirely of arms

Gathered like puppies with the children on the sofa

Game night   Friday night   Popcorn and a movie

Only falling into deep earned sleep

The List of Cloying Delights concludes with   a deep earned sleep

The List of Cloying Delights is composed entirely of hugging arms

Like many myths   it is a beautiful diaphanous useful type of net

Here I have captured myself up in it

✦

I had an ambition to make a book called *The Mother's Book*

It would be a short book containing inexorable truths

Like   an instruction manual   but also sage advice

I wanted to make something to give to women at the outset of the terrible journey

I mean   No   At the outset of a lonely voyage

But I had no advice   And each woman is a lone figure traveling across her own continent

✦

Waking inside a bouquet of arms the mother disappears among them

✦

Each woman is a lone figure traveling across her own continent

Snow or wet leaves or light glancing off glass

Or linoleum or red clay tile or the specific aroma of a green or amber
or purple cleaning product

Each woman is a lone figure traveling across her own continent

Here she is washing her dishes

Here she is washing another woman's dishes

Here another woman is washing her dishes

She plates food in the kitchen of the restaurant full of steam

That cavernous sink

The mother folds the towels into a neat rectangle

The woman removes her identity and folds it into a neat rectangle

Opening a book   Playing a movie

Taking a walk in a sack of loose baggy garments

The woman removes her hide and leaves it elsewhere for a while

✦

Passing through the pelvic bone as if passing through the world's gate

At what other point does one pass through a doorway of bone

The child is carried as if it were a heavy sack of glowing satin

Emily, the world said sweetly, curling its finger across my face, arms like earth beneath the length of my head and back

Passing through the pelvic bone   It was freezing in November

Heavily against her shoulder I rested the weight of my brand-new face

I was carried   She was tired   I was warm

Hera

Hera (the goddess) is a figure of vengeance

A queen who has power / who lacks power

A woman with the righteous rage of being wronged

A woman who wrongs

Twisting the figures of other women into the wrong forms

✦

Hera (my daughter) fetches her shoes

Hera (my daughter) pulls a book from her shelf

Hera as austere as a column in her pink cotton dress

Hera in her brothers' hand-me-downs doing the ordinary work
of being a child

Climbing the climber again and again

Hera in a myth that has not yet been thought of

In which she will neither wrong nor be wronged

History enters a new loop

✦

The Greek goddesses are like
a woman who has been divided into different portions

Of which Hera (the goddess) is the least appealing

Persephone is the period in which a girl grows up

Demeter the mother who wanted to preserve her

Artemis wants nothing to do with men

Aphrodite is a woman's beauty

Athena, wisdom stepping from a forehead

Hera schemes and seethes

Hera, imprisoned by her husband in golden chains
and pinned into the sky

✦

Hera (my daughter) lifts up her eyes like two pieces of ice

Like two blue flowers

Not flowers   Her eyes are the means with which she sees the world

✦

List of things into which Zeus transforms himself in order to
seduce / rape / please / abduct / trick / fuck

A mist of rain (gold) falling through the bars of a prison

A cloud

An eagle

A swan

A bull

Artemis (the goddess)

An injured cuckoo

✦

This last is the ruse he uses to first trick Hera
into bringing him into her arms

✦

The most common depiction of Hera
is in the painting *The Judgement of Paris*, thousands of versions exist

In it, Paris awards the golden apple to "she who is most lovely"

For the painter, "it allowed him to display his ideal of female beauty"

Most often the composition includes a shepherd (Paris)
gazing toward three nude women (Hera, Athena, Aphrodite)

(The women's bodies are pillars of milk)

(Smooth milk or sinewy milk or rumpled milk)

Hera is identified by a peacock; Athena a helmet; Aphrodite a dove

Etc etc

Coyly or playfully or half-covering-up

(Here is a myth)   (Or a truth)

(Women disrobing with alacrity to satisfy their own vanity)

I have given myself the task of submerging into pure patriarchy

I mean to emerge with something else

✦

"To oppose something is to maintain it" writes Ursula K. Le Guin in *The Left Hand of Darkness*

✦

Some quick myths of Hera

Hera blinds Tiresias

Hera curses Echo for deceiving her

Hera casts her son Hephaestus down from heaven

He makes a golden throne with invisible tethers to trap her inside it

When implored to free her, he says:

"I have no mother"

Etc etc

✦

Antonio da Vendri painted the version of *The Judgement of Paris*
that I like best

(Venice circa 1500–1524)

Here we see only heads and shoulders, hands

The woman whose back is to us wears a beaded trinzale in her hair

Velvet feathers fur / satin leather pearls

At the right Paris in a flat cap holds the golden apple

The women are dressed in expensive clothing

Standing close in a group of four, the women look to Paris, *who looks to us*

Through the frame of the painting   into our eyes

.   .   .

And what do we think?

✦

Hera (my daughter) joins me as I sweep

Carries laundry to the washer

(Uses a miniature broom, pushes a miniature basket of laundry)

Hera in a photo like a child from a painting

Stares impassively from her mother's (my) arms

Not impassive   Protected / contented / secure   Nobody's domain

✦

"Aegis-holder and queenly Hera of Argos who walks on golden sandals"

"Hera, the good wife of Zeus"

"white-armed Hera"

"gold-shod Hera"

"gold-throned Hera"

"large-eyed queenly Hera"

✦

Conditions that prompt Hera's fury:

    (1) An insult to her beauty

    (2) Zeus's indiscretions

If beauty and marriage comprise the bulk of a woman's power

If they encompass the whole of her security

Therefore

Picture a wife who is no longer pretty

Words like "sack" and "flaps" and "bulge" and "back"

A wife is so busy, her flesh slides down to the floor

✦

(Or)   (Beauty isn't power)

(It's more like another portal through which danger climbs)

(A window that stays open all night)

✦

Hera (my daughter) needs to have her fingernails cut

She snatches her hand away   (Her hand belongs to her)

I wait for her to proffer her hand

The girl remains owner of the girl's hand

✦

List of things Hera (the goddess) transforms women into

A bear

A crane

A voice who repeats the words of others

Little birds

Stones

To those most like her, Hera is a warning
To the husband, Hera is a warning
To the girl on the side, Hera is a warning

"I will make you yourselves tremendous memorials of my displeasure"

✦

Andrés says Hera the girl and Hera the goddess have nothing in common

That's true

Hera the goddess is a story told by men, about wives

Hera the girl is a person

✦

Hera the goddess is a story told by men, about wives

Happy wife, happy life, they say ruefully

Boys will be boys, they say ruefully

Hera is "odious" the philologist writes

While Zeus is "perhaps too good-natured"

Hera was jealous

Hera was difficult

Hera the repository of complaints

✦

Hera's power leaks out through this shape: Wife

✦

Dorothy (my grandmother)

Wearing fur coats from Sakowitz
Visiting Mickey Gilley's nightclub in snakeskin cowboy boots
Long beaded necklaces tinkling to her waist
Fine clothes
Deep nights
Hand-embroidered caftans from Morocco
The sky begins to lighten and brighten into birdsong-early gray

One afternoon she drove by the hotel
where my grandfather and his mistress stayed

"I only stayed in the parking lot long enough for them to see me.
Then I drove off."

Hera (the grandmother)
Chin lifted
Fingers interlaced across her chest
Diamonds arranged into the shape of Texas
Engagement ring reset into a "toi et moi" pearl and diamond
locked in an embrace

Two disparate stones twisted by metal into an eternal embrace

A lingering symbol   The private joke of a cast-off woman

✦

There are several paintings of Hera that I like

Example:

Paolo Veronese *Juno Showering Gifts on Venetia* circa 1554–1556
Picture pinks and golds swirling in a column of clouds
Between clouds and earth, a painfully blue sky

Hera (atop) carelessly drops tinkling gifts to the city of her patronage
Coins   Crowns   Twisted olive

What did Dorothy call herself in later years?
"A sugar mama"   (she says, smiling)
Smiling as if sitting atop a pile of coins

✦

Hera (the girl) arrived on Earth and entered a landscape of stories

Each story was like a tunnel through which to pass through life

Girl-shaped tunnels, boy-shaped tunnels, tunnels shaped like money

I do not like these tunnels, Hera may think

It is very difficult to make a new tunnel

(One must enter a tunnel, or make one)

✦

Of Mrs. Dickens,
Robert Gottlieb, the Charles Dickens family biographer, writes:

"Catherine represented all the messy business of life—
sex, childbirth, ill health"

Catherine bore Dickens 10 children

He then left her for an 18-year-old mistress

You may or may not know what it's like to bear a child

(physically)

✦

The messy business of life
Blood and falling organs

Hera the goddess of giving birth

My children weighed 5 lbs   7 lbs   10 lbs, respectively

For reference think of corresponding bags of flour

To give you an idea of the size and weight

The shape passing through

✦

"I will make you yourselves tremendous memorials of my displeasure"

is something I would like to say, sometimes

✦

Goddess of menstruation
Goddess of childbirth
Goddess of infertility
Goddess of the episiotomy
Goddess of colostrum
Goddess of meconium
Goddess of sutures
Goddess of gushing, pulsing, seeping, and leaking
Goddess of new hair dark like a seal's wet pelt
Goddess of a cooing little voice
Of shaking miniature cries

Goddess of marriage
Goddess of the wandering eye
Goddess of loose hair and discolored skin
Goddess of seething dishes, simmering skin
Goddess of dishes and thinning hair
Dishes. Trousers that no longer button.
Melodramatic laundry, fallen in melodramatic piles

✦

Hera (the girl) in her pink hair tie and pink bubble romper

Hera (the girl) sweeping with a miniature broom

Hera (the girl) wearing her name like an ancient epithet

Pony-tailed Hera
Nimble-footed Hera
Hera in a column of power

✦

Free internet encyclopedias describe Hera variously as

Jealous

Vengeful

Rancorous

Vindictive

I will make you yourselves
tremendous memorials of my displeasure
she says   gesturing toward the horizon of skyscrapers and freeways
toward the men who poison the air
toward the women who nibble the cast-off power of men
toward the bourgeois egos eating up the earth

✦

One must enter a tunnel, or make one

✦

A final myth to end things

After Argos is slain, Hera collects his hundred eyes
and pins them to the tail of a peacock

(Rubens depicts this)

(In the painting Hera in a crimson scarlet gown works impassively,
a collection of flat eyes in her right hand,
flat eyes loosely falling from her left)

This is my favorite myth of Hera because it has no clear symbology

In it a woman makes an odd thing to please herself alone

Acknowledgments

Acknowledgments are due to the editors of the following publications, in which some of these poems, or excerpts of them, first appeared: *bath magg*, *Copper Nickel*, Ruth Stone House's *Iterant*, *The Poetry Review*, and *Prelude*.

Credit to Yolanda Pantin, the title of whose long poem *El hueso pélvico* inspired me to write my own poem titled "The Pelvic Bone." And thank you to Denise Prince, whose photograph *Stack of Cakes* appears on the cover.

Gratitude to the artists whose work kept me company as I wrote this book:

Amy Boesky—*The Ghost Writes Back*
James M. Cain—*Mildred Pierce*
Audre Lorde—*The Black Unicorn*
Chelsey Minnis—*Bad Bad*
Doireann Ní Gríofa—*Mandible*
Yolanda Pantin—*Bellas Ficciones*
James Schuyler—*Hymn to Life*
Elliott Smith—*Either/Or*
Thao & the Get Down Stay Down—*Temple*
Lars von Trier—*Melancholia*
Antonio Vivaldi—*The Four Seasons*
(And to Dara and Lina, thank you for your thoughts, streaming across continents and years.)

References

Barker, Wright. *Circe*. 1899. Cartwright Hall Art Gallery, Bradford, UK. https://artuk.org/discover/artworks/circe-23017.

Bible. New Century Version. Nashville: Thomas Nelson, 2005.

Boucher, François. *Jupiter in the Guise of Diana, and the Nymph Callisto*. 1759. Nelson-Atkins Museum of Art, Kansas City, MO. https:// nelson-atkins.org/fpc/eighteenth-century-pre-revolution/306/.

Chopin, Kate. *The Awakening*. Chicago: Herbert S. Stone, 1899.

Correggio, Antonio Allegri. *Abduction of Ganymede*. ca. 1530. Kunsthistorisches Museum Vienna, Gemäldegalerie. https://www.khm.at/de/object/41/.

Correggio, Antonio Allegri. *Danaë*. ca. 1530–31. Galleria Borghese, Rome. https://www.collezionegalleriaborghese.it/en/opere/danae.

Correggio, Antonio Allegri. *Jupiter and Io*. ca. 1530. Kunsthistorisches Museum Vienna, Gemäldegalerie. https://www.khm.at/de/object/40/.

Correggio, Antonio Allegri. *Leda and the Swan*. ca. 1532. Staatliche Museen zu Berlin, Gemäldegalerie. https://id.smb.museum/object/862455/leda-mit-dem-schwan.

da Vendri, Antonio (attributed). *The Judgment of Paris*. 1500–1524. Rijksmuseum, Amsterdam. http://hdl.handle.net/10934/RM0001.collect.7254.

Delany, Mary. *Papaver Rheus*, formerly in an album (Vol.VII, 47); Common Corn Poppy. 1779. Collage of coloured papers, with bodycolour and watercolour, on black ink background. The British

Museum, London. https://www.britishmuseum.org/collection/
object/P_1897-0505-647.

Delany, Mary. *Passiflora Laurifolia (Gynandria Pentandria)*, formerly in an
album (Vol.VII, 54); Bay Leaved. 1777. Collage of coloured papers,
with bodycolour and watercolour, on black ink background. The
British Museum, London. https://www.britishmuseum.org/collection/
object/P_1897-0505-654

"Fanny Eaton." Wikipedia. Accessed October 7, 2020. https://
en.wikipedia.org/wiki/Fanny_Eaton.

Frey, Angelica. "The Women of Pre-Raphaelite Art." *Art & Object*,
November 4, 2020. https://www.artandobject.com/articles/women-
pre-raphaelite-art.

Gottlieb, Robert. *Great Expectations: The Sons and Daughters of Charles
Dickens*. New York: Picador, 2013.

Hawksley, Lucinda. "The Tragedy of Art's Greatest Supermodel." BBC,
July 31, 2020. https://www.bbc.com/culture/article/20200103-the-
tragedy-of-arts-greatest-supermodel.

"Hera." *Greek & Roman Mythology – Tools*. Accessed July 20, 2024.
https://www2.classics.upenn.edu/myth/php/tools/dictionary.
php?method=did&regexp=989&setcard=0&link=0&media=1.

Homer and Hesiod. *Hesiod, The Homeric Hymns, and Homerica*. Edited
by Hugh G. Evelyn-White. 1914. http://www.gutenberg.org/
files/348/348-h/348-h.htm#linknote-2102.

Hoyle, Arthur. *The Unknown Henry Miller: A Seeker in Big Sur*. New York:
Arcade, 2014.

"The Judgement of Paris." Flemish and Northern European Paintings
Department, Museo del Prado, March 2015. http://www.
museodelprado.es/en/the-collection/art-work/the-judgement-of-paris/
f8b061e1-8248-42ae-81f8-6acb5b1d5a0a.

"June Miller." Wikipedia. Accessed September 13, 2020. https://
en.wikipedia.org/wiki/June_Miller.

"Late Bloomer: The Exquisite Craft of Mary Delany." *The British Museum
Blog*, March 20, 2019. https://blog.britishmuseum.org/late-bloomer-
the-exquisite-craft-of-mary-delany/.

Le Guin, Ursula K. *The Left Hand of Darkness*. New York: Ace Books, 1969.

Light, Alan. "Ballad of the 13-Year-Old Bride." *Medium*, May 1, 2017. https://medium.com/cuepoint/ballad-of-the-13-year-old-bride-f909cbe1c6b4.

Lowell, Amy. "Granadilla." In *Ballads for Sale*. New York: Houghton Mifflin, 1927.

Lumb, Thomas Wallace. *Authors of Greece*. Port Washington, NY: Kennikat Press, 1969. http://www.gutenberg.org/files/8115/8115-h/8115-h.htm.

"Maria Clara Eimmart." Wikipedia. Accessed July 5, 2020. https://en.wikipedia.org/wiki/Maria_Clara_Eimmart.

Marsh, Jan. *Pre-Raphaelite Sisterhood*. London: Quartet Books, 1985.

Marsh, Jan, et al. *Pre-Raphaelite Sisters*. London: National Portrait Gallery Publications, 2019.

Mazza, Damiano. *The Rape of Ganymede*. ca. 1575. The National Gallery, London. https://www.nationalgallery.org.uk/paintings/damiano-mazza-the-rape-of-ganymede.

Millais, Sir John Everett. *Ophelia*. 1851–52. Tate, London. https://www.tate.org.uk/art/artworks/millais-ophelia-n01506.

"Mrs Delany's Petticoat." *The Gardens Trust*, July 7, 2018. https://thegardenstrust.blog/2018/07/07/mrs-delanys-petticoat/.

Niccol, Andrew. *The Truman Show*. 1998.

Opie, John. Mary Delany (née Granville). 1782. National Portrait Gallery, London. https://www.npg.org.uk/collections/search/portrait/mw01784/Mary-Delany-ne-Granville.

Ovid. *The Metamorphoses of Ovid*. Translated by Henry T. Riley. London: George Bell & Sons, 1893. http://www.gutenberg.org/files/21765/21765-h/main.html.

Rhys, Jean. *Good Morning, Midnight.* London: Constable, 1939.

"Room by Room: A Home Brought to Life." *Mark Twain House*, April 21, 2020. https://marktwainhouse.org/about/the-house/interior-grounds/rooms/.

"Rose La Touche." Wikipedia. Accessed March 1, 2019. https://en.wikipedia.org/wiki/Rose_La_Touche.

Rossetti, Dante Gabriel. *Lady Lilith*. 1866–68 (altered 1872–73). Delaware Art Museum, Delaware, MD. https://emuseum.delart.org/objects/6457/lady-lilith.

Rossetti, Dante Gabriel. *Veronica Veronese*. 1872. Delaware Art Museum, Delaware, MD. https://emuseum.delart.org/objects/321/veronica-veronese.

Rossetti, Dante Gabriel, and Henry Treffry Dunn. *Lady Lilith*. 1867. The Metropolitan Museum of Art, New York. https://www.metmuseum.org/art/collection/search/337500.

Rubens, Peter Paul. *The Judgement of Paris*. ca. 1638. Museo del Prado, Madrid. https://www.museodelprado.es/en/the-collection/art-work/the-judgement-of-paris/f8b061e1-8248-42ae-81f8-6acb5b1d5a0a.

Rubens, Peter Paul. *Juno and Argus*. ca. 1610. Wallraf-Richartz-Museum, Cologne. https://www.wallraf.museum/en/collections/baroque/masterpieces/peter-paul-rubens-juno-and-argus-c-1610/the-highlight/.

Ruskin, John. *Praeterita*. London: Allen and Unwin, 1907.

Serebriakova, Zinaida. *At the Dressing Table (Self-Portrait)*. 1909. Tretyakov Gallery, Moscow.

Sotheby's. "The Tragic Death of Dante Gabriel Rossetti's Ethereal Muse, Elizabeth Siddal." Sotheby's, June 17, 2019. https://www.sothebys.com/en/articles/the-tragic-death-of-dante-gabriel-rossettis-ethereal-muse-elizabeth-siddal.

Titian, Pieve di Cadore. *The Rape of Europa*. ca. 1559–62. Isabella Stewart Gardner Museum, Boston. https://www.gardnermuseum.org/experience/collection/10978.

TITLE VII—GENDER DISCRIMINATION—NINTH CIRCUIT HOLDS THAT WOMEN CAN BE FIRED FOR REFUSING TO WEAR MAKEUP.—Jespersen v. Harrah's Operating Co." *Harvard Law Review* 120, no. 2 (2006): 651–58. https://harvardlawreview.org/wp-content/uploads/pdfs/gender_discrimination_ninth_circuit.pdf.

Unknown. *Bust of Queen Nefertiti*. ca. 1345 BCE. From Amarna, now Neues Museum, Berlin. https://id.smb.museum/object/606189/büste-der-königin-nofretete.

Unknown. *Portrait of Livia, the Wife of Emperor Augustus.* ca. 14–29 CE. From Rome, now Hermitage Museum, Petersburg, Russia. https://hermitagemuseum.org/wps/portal/hermitage/digital-collection/06.+sculpture/188833.

Waterhouse, John William. *Circe Invidiosa.* 1892. Art Gallery of South Australia, Adelaide. https://www.agsa.sa.gov.au/collection-publications/collection/works/circe-invidiosa/24983/.

Waterhouse, John William. *Circe Offering the Cup to Ulysses.* 1891. Gallery Oldham, Oldham, UK. https://artuk.org/discover/artworks/circe-offering-the-cup-to-ulysses-90979.

Waterhouse, John William. *The Magic Circle.* 1886. Tate, London, UK. https://www.tate.org.uk/art/artworks/waterhouse-the-magic-circle-n01572.

Wells, Joanna Mary (née Boyce). *Fanny Eaton.* 1861. Yale Center for British Art, New Haven, CT. https://collections.britishart.yale.edu/catalog/tms:1336.

Wharton, Edith. *The House of Mirth.* New York: Charles Scribner's Sons, 1905.

Witt, Emily. "Daddy Issues: On the Worthless Brood of Charles Dickens." *Observer,* December 4, 2012. https://observer.com/2012/12/daddy-issues-on-the-worthless-brood-of-charles-dickens/.

Veronese, Paolo. *Juno Showering Gifts on Venetia.* ca. 1554–56. Doge's Palace, Venice. https://palazzoducale.visitmuve.it/en/the-museum/layout-and-collections/institutional-chambers/second-floor/.

WISCONSIN POETRY SERIES

SEAN BISHOP AND JESSE LEE KERCHEVAL, SERIES EDITORS

RONALD WALLACE, FOUNDING SERIES EDITOR

How the End First Showed (B) • D. M. Aderibigbe

New Jersey (B) • Betsy Andrews

Salt (B) • Renée Ashley

(At) Wrist (B) • Tacey M. Atsitty

Horizon Note (B) • Robin Behn

What Sex Is Death? (T) • Dario Bellezza, selected and translated by Peter Covino

About Crows (FP) • Craig Blais

Mrs. Dumpty (FP) • Chana Bloch

Rich Wife (4L) • Emily Bludworth de Barrios

Shopping, or The End of Time (FP) • Emily Bludworth de Barrios

The Declarable Future (4L) • Jennifer Boyden

The Mouths of Grazing Things (B) • Jennifer Boyden

Help Is on the Way (4L) • John Brehm

No Day at the Beach • John Brehm

Sea of Faith (B) • John Brehm

Reunion (FP) • Fleda Brown

Brief Landing on the Earth's Surface (B) • Juanita Brunk

Ejo: Poems, Rwanda, 1991–1994 (FP) • Derick Burleson

Grace Engine • Joshua Burton

The Roof of the Whale Poems (T) • Juan Calzadilla, translated by Katherine M. Hedeen and Olivia Lott

Jagged with Love (B) • Susanna Childress

Salvage • Hedgie Choi

Almost Nothing to Be Scared Of (4L) • David Clewell

The Low End of Higher Things • David Clewell

Now We're Getting Somewhere (FP) • David Clewell

Taken Somehow by Surprise (4L) • David Clewell

Thunderhead • Emily Rose Cole

(B) = Winner of the Brittingham Prize in Poetry

(FP) = Winner of the Felix Pollak Prize in Poetry

(4L) = Winner of the Four Lakes Prize in Poetry

(T) = Winner of the Wisconsin Prize for Poetry in Translation

EMILY BLUDWORTH DE BARRIOS is a poet whose previous book, *Shopping, or The End of Time*, received the Felix Pollak Prize in Poetry. Her poems have appeared in publications such as *Harvard Review*, *Copper Nickel*, *The Poetry Review*, and *Oxford Poetry*. She received her MFA from the University of Massachusetts at Amherst and also holds degrees from Goldsmiths College and the College of William & Mary. She was raised in Houston, Cairo, and Caracas, and now lives in Houston, Texas, and Santa Cruz de la Sierra, Bolivia.